HERAKLEITOS AND DIOGENES

The Intelligence of Louis Agassiz
Carmina Archilochi
Sappho: Songs and Fragments
Flowers and Leaves
Cydonia Florentia
Tatlin!
Da Vinci's Bicycle

HERAKLEITOS

Translated from the Greek by Guy Davenport

& DIOGENES

GREY FOX PRESS • BOLINAS • CALIFORNIA

"Herakleitos: The Extant Fragments" was published in *Contemporary Literature in Translation* No. 23 (Spring 1976), and reprinted in *The American Poetry Review* Vol. 7, No 1 (January/February 1978).

The cover drawing by Guy Davenport quotes a greyhound in marble from the Acropolis Museum, Athens, and a head in bronze by Julio Gonzales.

Book design and composition by Wesley B. Tanner.

LIBRARY OF CONGRESS CATALOGING IN PUBLICATION DATA

Herakleitos and Diogenes.

1. Aphorisms and apothegms.   I. Heraclitus, of Ephesus.   II. Diogenes, the Cynic.   III. Davenport, Guy.
PN6269.H4   182'.4   78-17310
ISBN 0-912516-35-6
ISBN 0-912516-36-4 pbk.

For Steven Diamant

ἄριστος συνεταῖρος καὶ ὁ φίλιστος

HERAKLEITOS

HERAKLEITOS. *Of Herakleitos we know only that he lived in Ephesos between 540 and 480 BC, and that he wrote a book dedicated to Artemis, fragments of which have survived through quotation by later writers.*

The astuteness and comprehensiveness of his insight into the order of nature have commanded attention for 2500 years, exhibiting a freshness for every generation. Plato counted him among the transcendent intelligences, as did Nietzsche, Gassendi, Niels Bohr, Spengler. His presence as a spirit in both modern poetry (Eliot, Pound, William Carlos Williams, Hopkins) and modern physics makes him peculiarly a twentieth-century guide, one of our daimons.

There are many studies of Herakleitos, and many translations. This one hopes merely to provide the simplest and most transparent English equivalent for the Greek that I can.

In Fragment 69 I have departed from literalness and accepted the elegant paraphrase of Novalis, "Character is fate." The Greek says that ethos is man's daimon: the moral climate of a man's cultural complex (strictly, his psychological weather) is what we mean when we say daimon, or guardian angel. As the daimons inspire and guide, character is the cooperation between psyche and daimon. The daimon has foresight, the psyche is blind and timebound. A thousand things happen to us daily which we sidestep or do not even notice. We follow the events which we are characteristically predisposed to cooperate with, designing what happens to us: character is fate.

9

The Logos is eternal
but men have not heard it
and men have heard it and not understood.

Through the Logos all things are understood
yet men do not understand
as you shall see when you put acts and words to the test
I am going to propose:

One must talk about everything according to its nature,
how it comes to be and how it grows.
Men have talked about the world without paying attention
to the world or to their own minds,
as if they were asleep or absent-minded.

. 2 .

Let us therefore notice that understanding is common to all
men. Understanding is common to all, yet each man acts as
if his intelligence were private and all his own.

. 3 .

Men who wish to know about the world must learn about
it in its particular details.

· 4 ·

Men dig up and search through much earth to find gold.

· 5 ·

Our understanding of the greatest matters will never be complete.

. 6 .

Knowledge is not intelligence.

· 7 ·

I have heard many men talk, but none who realized that understanding is distinct from all other knowledge.

. 8 .

I have looked diligently at my own mind.

· 9 ·

It is natural for man to know his own mind and to be sane.

Sanity is the highest excellence. The skillful mind speaks the truth, knowing how everything is separate in its own being.

I honor what can be seen, what can be heard, what can be learned.

Eyes are better informers than ears.

Eyes and ears are poor informers to the barbarian mind.

One ought not to talk or act as if he were asleep.

We share a world when we are awake; each sleeper is in a world of his own.

. 16 .

Awake, we see a dying world; asleep, dreams.

. 17 .

Nature loves to hide. [Becoming is a secret process].

(. 18 .)

The Lord who prophesies at Delphoi neither speaks clearly nor hides his meaning completely; he gives one symbols instead.

. 19 .

In searching out the truth be ready for the unexpected, for it is difficult to find and puzzling when you find it.

. 20 .

Everything flows; nothing remains. [Everything moves; nothing is still. Everything passes away; nothing lasts.]

. 21 .

One cannot step twice into the same river, for the water into which you first stepped has flowed on.

. 22 .

Cold things become hot; hot things, cold. Wet things, dry; dry things, wet.

. 23 .

Change alone is unchanging.

. 24 .

History is a child building a sand-castle by the sea, and that child is the whole majesty of man's power in the world.

. 25 .

War is the father of us all and our king. War discloses who is godlike and who is but a man, who is a slave and who is freeman.

. 26 .

It must be seen clearly that war is the natural state of man. Justice is contention. Through contention all things come to be.

. 27 .

When Homer said that he wished war might disappear from the lives of gods and men, he forgot that without opposition all things would cease to exist.

Everything becomes fire, and from fire everything is born, as in the eternal exchange of money and merchandise.

. 29 .

This world, which is always the same for all men, neither god nor man made: it has always been, it is, and always shall be: an everlasting fire rhythmically dying and flaring up again.

. 30 .

Not enough and too much.

. 31 .

Divides and rejoins, goes forward and then backward.

. 32 .

The first metamorphosis of fire is to become the sea, and half of the sea becomes the earth, half the flash of lightning.

. 33 .

As much earth is washed into the sea as sea-stuff dries and becomes part of the shore.

The life of fire comes from the death of earth. The life of
air comes from the death of fire. The life of water comes
from the death of air. The life of earth comes from the
death of water.

· 35 ·

Lightning is the lord of everything.

· 36 ·

There is a new sun for every day.

· 37 ·

The sun is one foot wide.

· 38 ·

If there were no sun, all the other stars together could not
dispell the night.

· 39 ·

Morning is distinguished from evening by the Bear who
rises and sets diametrically across from the path of Zeus of
the Burning Air.

· 40 ·

The most beautiful order of the world is still a random gathering of things insignificant in themselves.

· 41 ·

All beasts are driven to pasture.

· 42 ·

No matter how many ways you try, you cannot find a boundary to consciousness, so deep in every direction does it extend.

· 43 ·

The stuff of the psyche is a smoke-like substance of finest particles that gives rise to all other things; its particles are of less mass than any other substance and it is constantly in motion: only movement can know movement.

· 44 ·

The psyche rises as a mist from things that are wet.

· 45 ·

The psyche grows according to its own law.

18

. 46 .

A dry psyche is most skilled in intelligence and is brightest in virtue.

. 47 .

The psyche lusts to be wet [and to die].

. 48 .

A drunk man, staggering and mindless, must be led home by his son, so wet is his psyche.

. 49 .

Water brings death to the psyche, as earth brings death to water. Yet water is born of earth, and the psyche from water.

. 50 .

That delicious drink, spiced hot Pramnian wine mixed with resin, roasted barley, and grated goat's cheese, separates in the bowl if it is not stirred.

. 51 .

It is hard to withstand the heart's desire, and it gets what it wants at the psyche's expense.

· 52 ·

If every man had exactly what he wanted, he would be no better than he is now.

· 53 ·

Hide our ignorance as we will, an evening of wine reveals it.

· 54 ·

The untrained mind shivers with excitement at everything it hears.

· 55 ·

The stupid are deaf to truth: they hear, but think that the wisdom of a perception always applies to someone else.

· 56 ·

Bigotry is the disease of the religious.

· 57 ·

Many people learn nothing from what they see and experience, nor do they understand what they hear explained, but imagine that they have.

. 58 .

If everything were smoke, all perception would be by smell.

. 59 .

In Hades psyches perceive each other by smell alone.

. 60 .

The dead body is useless even as manure.

. 61 .

Men are not intelligent, the gods are intelligent.

. 62 .

The mind of man exists in a logical universe but is not itself logical.

. 63 .

The gods' presence in the world goes unnoticed by men who do not believe in the gods.

. 64 .

Man, who is an organic continuation of the Logos, thinks
he can sever that continuity and exist apart from it.

. 65 .

At night we extinguish the lamp and go to sleep; at death
our lamp is extinguished and we go to sleep.

. 66 .

Gods become men; men become gods, the one living the
death of the other, the other dying the life of the one.
[Wheelwright translates: Immortals become mortals,
mortals become immortals; they live in each other's death
and die in each other's life.]

. 67 .

In death men will come upon things they do not expect,
things utterly unknown to the living.

. 68 .

We assume a new being in death: we become protectors of
the living and the dead.

. 69 .

Character is fate.

· 70 ·

The greater the stakes, the greater the loss. [The more one puts oneself at the mercy of chance, the more chance will involve one in the laws of necessity and inevitability.]

· 71 ·

Justice stalks the liar and the false witness.

· 72 ·

Fire catches up with everything, in time.

· 73 ·

How can you hide from what never goes away?

· 74 ·

There are gods here, too.

· 75 ·

They pray to statues of gods and heroes much as they would gossip with the wall of a house, understanding so little of gods and heroes.

. 76 .

Paraders by night, magicians, Bacchantes, leapers to the flute and drum, initiates in the Mysteries — what men call the Mysteries are unholy disturbances of the peace.

· 77 ·

Their pompous hymns and phallic songs would be obscene if we did not understand that they are the rites of Dionysos. And Dionysos, through whom they go into a trance and speak in tongues and for whom they beat the drum, do they realize that he is the same god as Hades, Lord of the Dead?

. 78 .

They cleanse themselves with blood: as if a man fallen into the pigsty should wash himself with slop. To one who does not know what's happening, the religious man at his rites seems to be a man who has lost his mind.

· 79 ·

There is madness in the Sibyl's voice, her words are gloomy, ugly, and rough, but they are true for a thousand years, because a god speaks through her.

. 80 .

All men think.

. 81 .

All men should speak clearly and logically, and thus share
rational discourse and have a body of thought in common,
as the people of a city are all under the same laws. The laws
of men derive from the divine law, which is whole and
single, which penetrates as it will to satisfy human purposes,
but is mightier than any law known to men.

. 82 .

Defend the law as you would the city wall.

. 83 .

Law gives the people a single will to obey.

. 84 .

One man, to my way of thinking, is worth ten thousand, if
he's the best of his kind.

. 85 .

The best of men see only one thing worth having: undying
fame. They prefer fame to wealth. The majority of men
graze like cattle.

. 86 .

Those killed by Ares are honored by gods and men.

. 87 .

The man of greatest reputation knows how to defend a reputation.

. 88 .

Extinguish pride as quickly as you would a fire.

. 89 .

To do the same thing over and over is not only boredom: it is to be controlled by rather than to control what you do.

. 90 .

Dogs bark at strangers.

. 91 .

What do they have for intellect, for common sense, who believe the myths of the public singers and flock with the crowd as if public opinion were a teacher, forgetting that the many are bad, the few are good [there are many bad people, few good ones] ?

All men are equally mystified by unaccountable evidence, even Homer, wisest of the Greeks. He was mystified by children catching lice. He heard them say, What we have found and caught we throw away; what we have not found and caught we still have.

· 93 ·

Homer should be thrown out of the games and whipped, and Archilochos with him.

· 94 ·

Good days and bad days, says Hesiod, forgetting that all days are alike.

· 95 ·

The Ephesians might as well all hang themselves and let the city be governed by children. They have banished Hermadoros, best of their citizens, because they cannot abide to have among them a man so much better than they are.

· 96 ·

Ephesians, be rich! I cannot wish you worse.

· 97 ·

Life is bitter and fatal, yet men cherish it and beget children to suffer the same fate.

Opposites cooperate. The beautifullest harmonies come from opposition. All things repel each other.

We know health by illness, good by evil, satisfaction by hunger, leisure by fatigue.

Except for what things would we never have heard the word justice?

Sea water is both fresh and foul: excellent for fish, poison to men.

Asses would rather have hay than gold.

Pigs wash in mud, chickens in dust.

. 104 .

The handsomest ape is uglier than the ugliest man. The wisest man is less wise, less beautiful than a god: the distance from ape to man is that from man to god.

. 105 .

A boy is to a man as a man is to a god.

. 106 .

To God all is beautiful, good, and as it should be. Man must see things as either good or bad.

. 107 .

Having cut, burned and poisoned the sick, the doctor then submits his bill.

. 108 .

The same road goes both up and down.

. 109 .

The beginning of a circle is also its end.

. 110 .

The river we stepped into is not the river in which we stand.

. 111 .

Curled wool, straight thread.

. 112 .

Joints are and are not parts of the body. They cooperate through opposition, and make a harmony of separate forces. Wholeness arises from distinct particulars; distinct particulars occur in wholeness.

. 113 .

To live is to die, to be awake is to sleep, to be young is to be old, for the one flows into the other, and the process is capable of being reversed.

. 114 .

Hesiod, so wise a teacher, did not see that night and day are the same.

. 115 .

A bow is alive only when it kills.

. 116 .

The unseen design of things is more harmonious than the seen.

. 117 .

We do not notice how opposing forces agree. Look at the bow and the lyre.

. 118 .

Not I but the world says it: All is one.

. 119 .

Wisdom alone is whole, and is both willing and unwilling to be named Zeus.

. 120 .

Wisdom is whole: the knowledge of how things are plotted in their courses by all other things.

. 121 .

God is day night winter summer war peace enough too little, but disguised in each and known in each by a separate flavor.

. 122 .

The sun will never change the rhythm of its motion. If it did, the Erinyes, agents of justice, would bring it to trial.

. 123 .

All things come in seasons.

. 124 .

Even sleeping men are doing the world's business and helping it along.

DIOGENES

DIOGENES OF SINOPE. *Among the tombs that line the road into Corinth, Pausanias says in his* Travels, *you can see in a stand of cypress and pine near the city gate the grave of Diogenes of Sinope, the philosopher whom the Athenians called The Dog, "a Sokrates gone mad."*

He died at Corinth in his eighty-first year (some say ninetieth), a slave belonging to Xeniades, who bought him from the pirate Skirpalos (or, according to Cicero, Harpalus). "Sell me to that man," Diogenes had said at the slave market, "he needs a master." Diogenes had come up for sale when he was captured at sea, on his way to Aigina. In the world at that time, as now, kidnapping for ransom was a Mediterranean enterprise. Diogenes was a stray, a citizen of no city-state, a man without property or kin.

He seems to have welcomed slavery. He became the teacher of Xeniades' sons, a member of the family. "A benevolent spirit has entered my house," Xeniades said.

Diogenes was born in 404 BC in Sinope on the Black Sea, the modern Sinop in Turkey. His father, an official at the mint, was convicted of debasing the coinage, and the family was disgraced and exiled. Diogenes made his way to Athens, where he took up the jibe of being an outcast's son by saying that he, too, was a debaser of the coinage: meaning that, as a philosopher, his business was to assay custom and convention and sort the counterfeit from the solid currency.

He studied philosophy under Antisthenes, a crusty type who hated students, emphasized self-knowledge, discipline, and restraint, and held forth at a gymnasium

35

named *The Silver Hound in the old garden district out-
side the city. It was open to foreigners and the lower
classes, and thus to Diogenes. Wits of the time made a
joke of its name, calling its members stray dogs, hence
cynic (doglike), a label that Diogenes made into literal
fact, living with a pack of stray gods, homeless eycept for
a tub in which he slept. He was the Athenian Thoreau.*

All of Diogenes' writings are lost: some dialogues, a
Republic, *and his letters. What remain are his comments
as passed down through folklore to be recorded by vari-
ous writers. These have obviously been distorted, mis-
ascribed, and reworked. The ones I have chosen are from
Diogenes Laërtius and Plutarch.*

*He was a public scold, a pest, a licensed jester. He was
also powerfully influential as a moral and critical force.
It was at a school of Cynics in Tarsus that a Roman Jew
named Shaul Paulus learned to command rhetoric, logic,
and rigorous candor. We can even hear the sharp voice
of Diogenes in his turns of phrase. Diogenes had said that
the love of money was the metropolis of all evil; Paul,
that the love of money was the root of all evil.*

*Diogenes and Alexander the Great died on the same
day: a traditional belief that shows a curious affinity. Alexander said,"If I were not Alexander, I would be Diogenes," meaning, one supposes, that if he could not have
all of the world, he would have none of it. Neither knew
anything of compromise. They were perfect specimens
of their kind.*

*Athens in Diogenes' long life changed from the bril-
liant epoch of Euripides and Sophokles, to a city in the*

36

Alexandrian empire, soon to be replaced as the intellectual center by Alexandria. Sokrates drank the hemlock when he was five. Plato, aged 80, died when Diogenes was 57. He was 48 when Alexander was born, 68 when Alexander came to the throne. He was a contempory of Praxiteles, Skopas, and Apelles. He invented the word cosmopolitan, *to designate himself a citizen of the world.*

have come to debase the coinage.

. 2 .

All things belong to the gods. Friends own things in common. Good men are friends of the gods. All things belong to the good.

· 3 ·

Men nowhere, but real boys at Sparta.

· 4 ·

I am a yapping Maltese lap dog when hungry, a Molossian wolfhound when fed, breeds tedious to hunt with but useful for guarding the house and the sheepfold.

· 5 ·

No one can live with me as a companion: it would be too inconvenient.

39

. 6 .

It is absurd to bring back a runaway slave. If a slave can survive without a master, is it not awful to admit that the master cannot live without the slave?

· 7 ·

I am a citizen of the world.

. 8 .

We are not as hardy, free, or accomplished as animals.

· 9 ·

If only I could free myself from hunger as easily as from desire.

. 10 .

Of what use is a philosopher who doesn't hurt anybody's feelings?

. 11 .

Demosthenes is a Scythian in his speeches and a gentleman on the battlefield.

. 12 .

The darkest place in the tavern is the most conspicuous.

. 13 .

I am Athens' one free man.

. 14 .

The porches and streets of Athens were built for me as a place to live.

. 15 .

I learned from the mice how to get along: no rent, no taxes, no grocery bill.

. 16 .

Plato winces when I track dust across his rugs: he knows that I'm walking on his vanity.

. 17 .

How proud you are of not being proud, Plato says, and I reply that there is pride and pride.

41

. 18 .

When I die, throw me to the wolves. I'm used to it.

. 19 .

A man keeps and feeds a lion. The lion owns a man.

. 20 .

The art of being a slave is to rule one's master.

. 21 .

Everything is of one substance. It is custom, not reason, that sets the temple apart from the house, mutton from human flesh for the table, bread from vegetable, vegetable from meat.

. 22 .

Antisthenes made me an exiled beggar dressed in rags: wise, independent, and content.

. 23 .

It is luckier to be a Megarian's ram than his son.

· 24 ·

Before begging it is useful to practice on statues.

· 25 ·

When the Sinopians ostracized me from Pontos, they condemned themselves to a life without me.

· 26 ·

Aristotle dines at King Philip's convenience, Diogenes at his own.

· 27 ·

When Plato said that if I'd gone to the Sicilian court as I was invited, I wouldn't have to wash lettuce for a living, I replied that if he washed lettuce for a living he wouldn't have had to go to the Sicilian court.

· 28 ·

Philosophy can turn a young man from the love of a beautiful body to the love of a beautiful mind.

· 29 ·

When I was captured behind the Macedonian lines and taken before Philip as a spy, I said that I'd only come to see how big a fool a king can be.

A. I am Alexander the Great.
B. I am Diogenes, the dog.
A. The dog?
B. I nuzzle the kind, bark at the greedy, and bite louts.
A. What can I do for you?
B. Stand out of my light.

To live is not itself an evil, as has been claimed, but to lead a worthless life is.

They laugh at me, but I'm not laughed at.

Great crowds at the Olympic games, but not of people.

The Shahinshah of Persia moves in pomp from Susa in the spring, from Babylon in the winter, from Media in the summer, and Diogenes walks every year from Athens to Corinth, and back again from Corinth to Athens.

I threw my cup away when I saw a child drinking from his hands at the trough.

. 36 .

Go into any whorehouse and learn the worthlessness of the expensive.

· 37 ·

We can only explain you, young man, by assuming that your father was drunk the night he begot you.

. 38 .

Can you believe that Pataikion the thief will fare better in Elysion because of his initiation into the Mysteries than Epameinondas the Pythagorean?

· 39 ·

One wrong will not balance another: to be honorable and just is our only defense against men without honor or justice.

. 40 .

To be saved from folly you need either kind friends or fierce enemies.

. 41 .

Watching a mouse can cure you of jealousy of others' good fortune.

· 42 ·

There is no stick hard enough to drive me away from a man from whom I can learn something.

· 43 ·

Eukleidos' lectures limp and sprawl, Plato's are tedious, tragedies are quarrels before an audience, and politicians are magnified butlers.

· 44 ·

Watch a doctor, philosopher, or helmsman, and you will conclude that man is the most intelligent of the animals, but then, regard the psychiatrist and the astrologer and their clients, and those who think they are superior because they are rich. Can creation display a greater fool than man?

· 45 ·

Reason or a halter.

· 46 ·

Why Syrakousa, friend Plato? Are not the olives in Attika just as toothsome?

· 47 ·

Plato's philosophy is an endless conversation.

Beg a cup of wine from Plato and he will send you a whole jar. He does not give as he is asked, nor answer as he is questioned.

· 49 ·

Share a dish of dried figs with Plato and he will take them all.

· 50 ·

Grammarians without any character at all lecture us on that of Odysseus.

· 51 ·

The contest that should be for truth and virtue is for sway and belongings instead.

· 52 ·

Happy the man who thinks to marry and changes his mind, who plans a voyage he does not take, who runs for office but withdraws his name, who wants to belong to the circle of an influential man, but is excluded.

· 53 ·

A friend's hand is open.

· 54 ·

Bury me prone: I have always faced the other way.

· 55 ·

Raising sons: teach them poetry, history, and philosophy. Geometry and music are not essential, and can be learned later. Teach them to ride a horse, to shoot a true bow, to master the slingshot and javelin. At the gymnasium they should exercise only so much as gives them a good color and a trim body. Teach them to wait upon themselves at home, and to enjoy ordinary food, and to drink water rather than wine. Crop their hair close. No ornaments. Have them wear a thin smock, go barefoot, be silent, and never gawk at people on the street.

. 56 .

In the rich man's house there is no place to spit but in his face.

· 57 ·

The luxurious have made frugality an affliction.

. 58 .

I'm turning that invitation down: the last time I was there, they were not thankful enough that I came.

· 59 ·

When some strangers to Athens asked me to show them Demosthenes, I gave them the finger, so that they would know what it felt like to meet him.

· 60 ·

A choirmaster pitches the note higher than he knows the choristers can manage. So do I.

· 61 ·

Go about with your middle finger up and people will say you're daft; go about with your little finger out, and they will cultivate your acquaintance.

· 62 ·

For three thousand drachmas you can get a statue, for two coppers a quart of barley.

· 63 ·

Masters should obey their slaves; patients, their doctors; rivers, their banks.

· 64 ·

Against fate I put courage; against custom, nature; against passion, reason.

. 65 .

Toadying extends even to Diogenes, I say to the mice who nibble my crumbs.

. 66 .

Even with a lamp in broad daylight I cannot find an honest man.

. 67 .

There are gods. How else explain people like Lysias the apothecary on whom the gods have so obviously turned their backs?

. 68 .

You can no more improve yourself by sacrificing at the altar than you can correct your grammar.

. 69 .

We are more curious about the meaning of dreams than about things we see when awake.

. 70 .

Pilfering Treasury property is particulary dangerous: big thieves are ruthless in punishing little thieves.

· 71 ·

It is not for charity but my salary that I beg in the streets.

· 72 ·

Had to lift its skirt to see whether man or woman had stopped me to talk philosophy.

· 73 ·

I pissed on the man who called me a dog. Why was he so surprised ?

· 74 ·

Pitching heeltaps: the better you are at it, the worse for you.

· 75 ·

You know the kind of luckless folk we call triple wretches. Well, these professors and others of that kidney who long to be known as famous lecturers are triple Greeks.

· 76 ·

The ignorant rich, sheep with golden fleeces.

· 77 ·

The athlete's brain, like his body, is as strong as that of a bull.

· 78 ·

Love of money is the marketplace for every evil.

· 79 ·

A good man is a picture of a god.

· 80 ·

Running errands for Eros is the business of the idle.

· 81 ·

The greatest misery is to be old, poor, and alone.

· 82 ·

The deadliest bite among wild animals is that of the boot-licker; amongst tame, that of the flatterer.

. 83 .

Choked on the honey of flattery.

. 84 .

The stomach is our life's Charybdis.

. 85 .

The golden Aphrodite that Phryne put up at Delphoi should be inscribed *Greek Lechery, Its Monument*.

. 86 .

A pretty whore is poisoned honey.

. 87 .

If, as they say, I am only an ignorant man trying to be a philosopher, then that may be what a philosopher is.

. 88 .

People who talk well but do nothing are like musical instruments: the sound is all they have to offer.

. 89 .

Aren't you ashamed, I said to the prissy young man, to assume a lower rank in nature than you were given?

. 90 .

Be careful that your pomade doesn't cause the rest of you to stink.

. 91 .

Why do we call house slaves footmen? Well, it's because they are men and they have feet.

. 92 .

What lovers really enjoy are their spats and the disapproval of society.

· 93 ·

Beggars get handouts before philosophers because people have some idea of what it's like to be blind and lame.

· 94 ·

If your cloak was a gift, I appreciate it; if it was a loan, I'm not through with it yet.

· 95 ·

Why praise Diokles for giving me a drachma and not me for deserving it?

. 96 .

I have seen the victor Dioxippos subdue all contenders at Olympia and be thrown on his back by the glance of a girl.

· 97 ·

To own nothing is the beginning of happiness.

. 98 .

Every day's a festival to the upright.

· 99 ·

Why not whip the teacher when the pupil misbehaves?

. 100 .

I had my lunch in the courtroom because that's where I was hungry.

. 101 .

It is a convenience not to fear the dark.

. 102 .

Discourse on virtue and they pass by in droves, whistle and dance the shimmy, and you've got an audience.

. 103 .

After grace and a prayer for health, the banqueters set to and eat themselves into an apoplexy.

. 104 .

To a woman who had flopped down before an altar with her butt in the air I remarked in passing that the god was also behind her.

. 105 .

At Khrysippos' lecture I saw the blank space coming up on the scroll, and said to the audience: Cheer up, fellows, land is in sight !

. 106 .

We have complicated every simple gift of the gods.

56

. 107 .

Make passes at you, do they? Why, then, don't you wear clothes that don't so accurately outline what they're interested in?

. 108 .

After a visit to the baths, where do you go to have a wash?

. 109 .

I've seen Plato's cups and table, but not his cupness and tableness.

. 110 .

If you've turned yourself out so handsomely, young man, for men, it's unfortunate; if for women, it's unfair.

. 111 .

A blush is the color of virtue.

. 112 .

A lecher is a fig tree on a cliff: crows get the figs.

. 113 .

The road from Sparta to Athens is like the passageway in a house from the men's rooms to the women's.

. 114 .

An obol now, friend, and when the community asks you to contribute for my funeral, you can say that you've already given.

. 115 .

I was once as young and silly as you are now, but I doubt if you will become as old and wise as I am.

. 116 .

Begging from fat Anaximenes, I argued what an advantage it would be to him to share the makings of that paunch with the poor.

. 117 .

There is no society without law, no civilization without a city.

. 118 .

The only real commonwealth is the whole world.

. 119 .

Practice makes perfect.

. 120 .

Learn the pleasure of despising pleasure.

. 121 .

Education disciplines the young, comforts the old, is the
wealth of the poor, and civilizes the rich.

. 122 .

The greatest beauty of humankind is frankness.

. 123 .

Plato begs too, but like Telemakhos conversing with Athe-
na, with lowered head, so that others may not overhear.

. 124 .

Give up philosophy because I'm an old man? It's at the end
of a race that you break into a burst of speed.

Photo by Guy Mendes

Guy Davenport has also translated the complete extant fragments of the Greek poets Archilochos, Sappho, and Alkman. He teaches at the University of Kentucky, lecturing on European Literature of the first half of the twentieth century, Joyce, Pound, and others. His work includes criticism, short stories, essays, poems, drawings and paintings.

GREY FOX PRESS BOOKS

Edward Dorn
Selected Poems

Allen Ginsberg
The Gates of Wrath: Rhymed Poems 1948-1952
Gay Sunshine Interview (with Allen Young)
Improvised on the Tongue

Jack Kerouac
Heaven & Other Poems

Michael McClure
Hymns to St. Geryon & Dark Brown

Frank O'Hara
Early Writing
Poems Retrieved
Standing Still and Walking in New York

Charles Olson
The Post Office

Gary Snyder
*He Who Hunted Birds in His Father's Village:
The Dimensions of a Haida Myth*

Gary Snyder, Lew Welch & Philip Whalen
On Bread & Poetry

Lew Welch
How I Work as a Poet & Other Essays/Plays/Stories
I, Leo — An Unfinished Novel
*I Remain: The Letters of Lew Welch & the
Correspondence of His Friends*
Ring of Bone: Collected Poems 1950-1971
Selected Poems
Trip Trap (with Jack Kerouac & Albert Saijo)

Philip Whalen
Decompressions: Selected Poems
Scenes of Life at the Capital